MW00581493

Josie's Passage

J.G. EASTWOOD

Photos Courtesy
J. G. Eastwood, Melissa Williford
& Debra Lienemann

Copyright © 2022 by J.G. Eastwood
jgeastwoodauthor.com

All rights reserved. No part of this publication may be reproduced, distributed, or transmitted in any form or by any means, including photocopying, recording, or other electronic or mechanical methods, without the prior written permission of the author, except in the case of brief quotations embodied in critical reviews and certain other noncommercial uses permitted by copyright law.

ISBN: 978-1-64314-714-7 (Paperback)

AuthorsPress
California, USA
www.authorspress.com

~ Acknowledgements ~

This book is dedicated to those who helped in the rescue
of an extraordinary dog…

Cumberland Animal Urgent Care, Fayetteville Police Department, Cumberland County Animal Control, Fayetteville, North Carolina, Founder & Director of Peak Lab Rescue (PLR), Debbie Letteney & the PLR team; Wendy Lodato, Sharon Gesser, Karen Steers, Lyn Craddock, Kristine Demko, Transporter for PLR, Jeff Lienemann, Apex, N.C., Foster Care PLR, Glenn & Melissa Williford, their granddaughter, Carson Williford, foster sibling, "Big Ben," Willow Spring, N.C., Chatham Animal Clinic in Virginia, Dr. Lisa Shorter, Dr. Victoria Shorter and Harmony Animal Hospital Apex North Carolina

Also…

For the many animal shelters, fosters, transporters and veterinarians who lend their resources, talents and time to insure that all dogs, which come into their care, will be given every opportunity to thrive and become healthy, happy and loving members of their adoptive families.

~ Foreword ~

Do not worry that you are not strong enough when you begin your journey.
It is during that passage God makes you strong.

"The Lord shall guide thee continually and satisfy thy soul."
Isaiah 58:11

~ Josie's Passage ~

A great story grips you at the beginning, holding you in suspense until its ending, one that you will never forget. But it is the passage in-between those times that makes a true story, a truly extraordinary story.

This true story is my extraordinary story. It begins when I was eight weeks old. I cannot tell you what happened in my life before then, and for now it will remain a mystery to those who helped me. I remembered what happened to me, but I couldn't share it. I do know that I was born a Labrador Retriever in Fayetteville, North Carolina.

At eight weeks old, I found myself in a dark, and desolate wooded area with no houses in sight. There I was, alone and frightened. I was cold and hungry, and, my left hind leg wasn't working right, and it hurt. As I looked around, I saw empty snack bags and drink cans, and other trash that had been thrown away. I remembered thinking…" Why was I thrown out? What was wrong with me?"

As I thought about it, I remembered before that I felt warm, loved, and my belly was full. I was so scared. I did not want to be here. I wanted to go back to before.

The dreary wintry day was getting dimmer and colder, and I was tired. I found a nest of leaves, so I tucked myself in.

As I struggled to keep warm, I could hear odd sounds all around me, and I saw strange creatures, which I had never seen before. I was alone for the first time in my life, and I didn't like it. I finally fell asleep, and I dreamed of home, and my mother and siblings.

It was a long night, but finally the morning came, and I was frozen, and so hungry. My leg was so cold, and it ached. I had to find something to eat, but the chip bags were empty, and the rest did not smell like food.

I did find some water, but it was frozen ice, and I couldn't drink it. I just licked it, and then my tongue was frozen.

I walked a little along the side of the road for a while, as cars and trucks passed by, I remembered then that I had been brought here in a truck, dumped and left on my own. The day passed, and it was getting dark, and I was cold, hungry and tired.

I felt so alone, and I whimpered and then I cried out.

As I searched for another warm place to spend another night, I felt a warming presence gently caressing me with invisible hands. Then, a soft light began to form above me, and it was wonderful. Though I didn't understand it, I liked the light. It swaddled me in warmth, easing the pain in my leg. As the light increased in warmth and brightness, in some way, it assured me that I would soon be home once more. I just had to keep going, and not give up.

Then, as the warm light was cuddling me, a car slowed down, and stopped not too far from where I was. As I looked on, the car stopped and two strangers got out, and approached me. They called me, and then I remembered that I had lived with beings like this before they brought me here. However, these were different. I liked them, and they liked me. One of them picked me up, and said, "I think she's hurt. Poor little puppy." "What should we do with her?" asked the other. "We can't take care of her; she needs medical help. I think it would be best if we take her to Cumberland Animal Urgent Care." the other replied, "I believe that place is open during the evening and night hours." The two agreed, and one held me in their lap while the other drove the car. It was good to be in someone's lap and being patted. As I looked out the car window, I could still see the beautiful light. Was it following me? I think it was following me.

Josie

Jeff Leineman

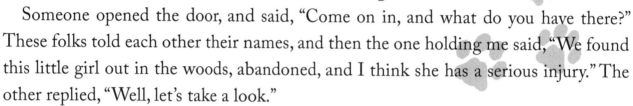

Finally, after a very long ride, the driver pulled into a parking lot of a place I had never seen. They stopped, and they got out of the car with me, and we went to the door of the building. They pushed a button and a bell rang.

I could feel something in my chest fluttering, and then I felt pounding.

I could not catch my breath. I trembled. I was frightened.

Someone opened the door, and said, "Come on in, and what do you have there?" These folks told each other their names, and then the one holding me said, "We found this little girl out in the woods, abandoned, and I think she has a serious injury." The other replied, "Well, let's take a look."

Then he said, " I will report this to the police department. This pup is cold, starving, and it appears her leg may be broken." I was checked over. My belly was distended and my tongue was pale. They put me on scales and said, I weighed 8 lbs. 2 oz. After checking me out, he said, "She has fleas, is anemic, and has intestinal parasites," whatever they are. I had plenty of things going on and because I couldn't bear weight on my left hind leg when I was standing, the man said it's probably fractured. I was treated, and given a shot for the pain.

Then, they told the people who brought me in that they were "Good Samaritans." The Good Samaritans gave their permission for me to go to Animal Control, where more folks would help me get to the places I needed to be. They were unprepared to pay for medical treatment, and had no intentions of adopting me. Then, the being telephoned the police department, and assured the friends who brought me in, that I would be okay. My "Good Samaritan" friends, waved good-bye to me, and they left.

They left me, and I became uneasy. I wanted to stay with them.

I could still see the light. It was peaking in the window, as the man put me in a crate with water and some food, and then he left me alone, too.

Kristine Dow Demko 🛡 Sasha is a 9 week old with a fractured femur. We are hoping we can save the leg. She has a battle ahead, but with a loving foster, we know she'll be okay!

Like · Reply · 34w ❤ 1

Later, after I had eaten, and settled in, the man got me out of the cage, and walked into the first room. Two new people, dressed in the same clothes, took me from the man who was taking care of me. These people were with the Fayetteville Police Department. I heard them say, "We'll see what we can do for this little girl. We will file a report, and call Cumberland Animal Control, in Fayetteville, and tell them we are bringing the pup to them."

The two people with the police department then took me in a car with all kinds of gadgets, and I was traveling again. They drove to another place and took me in to the building where there were a lot of new people. They were all busy doing different things. I arrived safely, and was now at Cumberland County Animal Control.

A nice lady, with a big smile, took me into her arms, and I liked the touch. She patted my head, rubbed my nose, gave me a hug, and said, "We are going to get you the help you need, little one, I promise."

Though I couldn't see the light, I sensed it, and I was going to be fine now. Then my new friends took pictures of my bad leg. They called the pictures X-rays. They filled out still another report, and took my picture with another man holding me. I was given a name; Animal A308003. I really didn't like that name.

My name was added to my reports. The folks phoned a place called Peak Lab Rescue in Apex, North Carolina. PLR committed to the final phase of my rescue during the phone call, and named me Sasha. And, now as Sasha Cumberland, because I was found in Cumberland County, I was posted on PLR Foster Families' Facebook. PLR said that they would send a transport to pick me up. My chest was feeling strange again, and I was so scared. Where was I going now, and what was going to happen next? I wondered if anyone would like me enough to keep me.

I waited for awhile, playing with these folks, when the man from Peak Lab Rescue finally arrived. He came to transport me to another place. He had a big smile, and was very happy to see me. They gave him my paperwork, he put me in his vehicle, and we were on the road again. He talked with me, and I liked him. The trip took a long time, but we finally arrived at a place called Harmony Animal Hospital in Apex, North Carolina. When we got out of his vehicle, I saw the light. It was still with me. The light was indeed following me where I went. My transporter, and I were welcomed by more people, all beaming big smiles. They were expecting me. The man who transported me then left.

It seemed nobody wanted to keep me. I remembered that the comforting light had found me in the woods, and stayed with me. The light followed me everywhere I went. Could anyone else see the light?

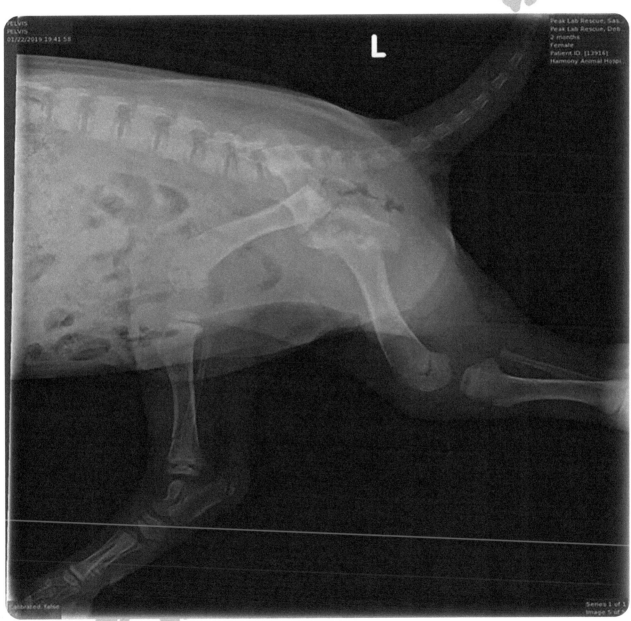

IDEXX

  SASHA CUMBERLAND PEAK LAB RESCUE

PET OWNER: **PEAK LAB RESCUE**	HARMONY ANIMAL HOSPITAL	LAB ID:	4501380038
SPECIES: Canine	2141 TEN TEN ROAD	ORDER ID:	38438209-C
BREED: LABRADOR_RETRIE	APEX, NC 27539	COLLECTION DATE: **1/22/19**
GENDER: Female	919-303-3456	DATE OF RECEIPT: **1/23/19**
AGE: 2 Months	ACCOUNT #: 22050	DATE OF RESULT: **1/23/19**
PATIENT ID: 13916	ATTENDING VET: AH,HARMONY		

IDEXX Services: **SAMPLE/TEST INFO NEEDED, Young Adult Profile**

Hematology

1/23/19 (Order Received)
1/23/19 2:29 AM (Last Updated)

TEST	RESULT	REFERENCE VALUE	
RBC	3.63	5.39 - 8.7 M/µL	L
Hematocrit	26.0	38.3 - 56.5 %	L
Hemoglobin	8.2	13.4 - 20.7 g/dL	L
MCV	72	59 - 76 fL	
MCH	22.6	21.9 - 26.1 pg	
MCHC	31.5	32.6 - 39.2 g/dL	L
% Reticulocyte	4.0	%	
Reticulocytes	145	10 - 110 K/µL	H

Reticulocyte Comment

The appropriateness of the regenerative response should be evaluated considering the degree of anemia and reticulocytosis (see guidelines below).

Degree of bone marrow response (reticulocytes K/uL):
Mild   110-150
Moderate 150-300
Marked   >300

View the VetConnect Plus Differentials for additional information.

TEST	RESULT	REFERENCE VALUE	
Reticulocyte Hemoglobin	24.3	22.3 - 29.6 pg	
WBC	12.4	4.9 - 17.6 K/µL	
% Neutrophils	40.2	%	
% Lymphocytes	43.1	%	
% Monocytes	8.4	%	
% Eosinophils	8.1	%	
% Basophils	0.2	%	
Neutrophils	4.985	2.94 - 12.67 K/µL	
Lymphocytes	5.344	1.06 - 4.95 K/µL	H
Monocytes	1.042	0.13 - 1.15 K/µL	
Eosinophils	1.004	0.07 - 1.49 K/µL	
Basophils	a 0.025	0 - 0.1 K/µL	

IDEXX

| | SASHA CUMBERLAND PEA... | PET OWNER: **PEAK LAB RESCUE** | DATE OF RESULT: **1/23/19** | LAB ID: 4501380038 |

Hematology (continued)

TEST	RESULT	REFERENCE VALUE	
Platelets	372	143 - 448 K/µL	

a AUTOMATED CBC

Chemistry

1/23/19 (Order Received)
1/23/19 2:29 AM (Last Updated)

TEST		RESULT	REFERENCE VALUE		
Glucose		144	63 - 114 mg/dL	H	
IDEXX SDMA	a	13	0 - 14 µg/dL		
Creatinine		0.5	0.5 - 1.5 mg/dL		
BUN		14	9 - 31 mg/dL		
BUN: Creatinine Ratio		28.0			
Total Protein		4.7	5.5 - 7.5 g/dL	L	
Albumin		2.5	2.7 - 3.9 g/dL	L	
Globulin		2.2	2.4 - 4.0 g/dL	L	
Albumin: Globulin Ratio		1.1	0.7 - 1.5		
ALT		14	18 - 121 U/L	L	
ALP		125	5 - 160 U/L		
Bilirubin - Total		0.1	0.0 - 0.3 mg/dL		
Hemolysis Index	b	N			
Lipemia Index	c	N			

a   BOTH SDMA AND CREATININE ARE WITHIN THE REFERENCE INTERVAL which indicates
kidney function is likely good. Evaluate a complete urinalysis and confirm
there is no other evidence of kidney disease.

b   Index of N, 1+, 2+ exhibits no significant effect on chemistry values.

c   Index of N, 1+, 2+ exhibits no significant effect on chemistry values.

IDEXX

🐕 SASHA CUMBERLAND PEA... PET OWNER: **PEAK LAB RESCUE** DATE OF RESULT: **1/23/19** LAB ID: 4501380038

Other

1/23/19 (Order Received)
1/23/19 2:29 AM (Last Updated)

TEST	RESULT
More Information Needed	A fecal specimen was not received. The remainder of requested testing has been performed. Thank you.

Phone: 919-303-3456
Fax: 919-249-5149
www.harmonyanimalhospital.net

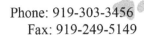

Patient Report Card

Owner: Debbie Letteney Peak Lab Rescue	01-23-19
Patient: Sasha Cumberland	Age: 9W
Today's weight: 7.98 lbs	Body Condition Score: 5 out of 9 (5 is ideal)

Today's testing and treatments:
Examination/Consultation - Rescue Group
Radiographs- Orthopedic Minor Series
Rescue Courtesy Discount (25%)
CBC, Chem 11 Idexx (12949999)
DECLINED: Fecal Examination w/ Centrifugation – no sample to collect
Microchip - provided by rescue group
PLR Flea/Tick Prev. Administered:
PLR HW Prev. Administered:
Courtesy Nail Trim Today (Value $18)
Courtesy Ear Cleaning (Value $20.40)

Today's diagnosis or problems:
FRACTURED LEFT FEMUR
POSSIBLE GREENSTICK FRACTURE Left distal tibia, nondisplaced
SWEET PUPPY
FEW CRUSTS AND SCABS – near vulva
NON-WEIGHT BEARING LEFT REAR LAMENESS

Recommendations:
Gender: Female   Color: Black   Spay/Neutered? Yes/No

_X_Exam- Abnormalities noted:

Vaccines administered today: Diagnostics done today:
__ Da2PP   __ Fecal exam
__ Rabies   __ Heartworm test
__ Bordetella   _X_ Other: CBC/Chem 11, Radiographs

Other items done today:
_X_Nail trim
_X_Microchip: # 956000010629121
__Dewormer administered:
__Capstar (If fleas present)
_X_Ears Cleaned
__BNT administered (If ear infection)
_X_HWP administered: Revolution

Phone: 919-303-3456
Fax: 919-249-5149
www.harmonyanimalhospital.net

_X_Flea/tick topical applied: Revolution

Next Visit Is due:
Sasha has an anemia and decreased albumin, total proteins on her labwork. We were not able to get a stool sample while she was here (empty). Please return a stool sample for fecal analysis as soon as you can. I suspect the most likely cause is intestinal parasitism, poor diet, malnutrition - please be sure she is eating puppy food well, add canned if needed to support appetite. Since the shelter dewormed with pyrantel on 1/20, we could deworm with an alternative dewormer (recommend Panacur x 3 days) or wait for fecal results and then decide. Next vaccines due in 3 weeks.
Per Dr. Taylor - We confirmed she has a femoral neck fracture in the left hip and a non displaced hairline fracture in the distal left tibia. We recommend crate rest for the next 2-4 weeks while monitoring her use of the leg. This will allow her to grow a bit more prior to pursuing an FHO on the left hip. If she is very uncomfortable, however, we may need to schedule this surgery as needed. She may continue on the Carprofen as directed until then. Please call with any concerns.

Thank you for entrusting Sasha Cumberland to our care. Please call us if you have any questions or concerns.

Thank you,
Laura Gaylord, DVM

The people at the hospital told me that I was being admitted for the care I needed. Some of the tests were repeated. The dog doctor said that I would need surgery on my left leg when I got older. I had a broken femur and a hairline fracture in the tibia; those are bones in my leg. She gave me pain medication, and it eased the hurting in my leg.

Then, after my name and photo posted to the PLR's Families Facebook page, Melissa and Glenn Williford, fosters with PLR, agreed to foster me and take care of me until, at which time, I would be adopted by a "fur-ever family." I liked the word, family. Could it happen, and when would it happen?

From January 19-22, 2019, I changed hands seven times from when the Good Samaritans first found me on the roadside in Cumberland County, North Carolina; Animal Urgent Care, Fayetteville Police, Cumberland County Animal Control, Jeff Lienemann, Harmony Animal Hospital, and last, Glenn and Melissa Williford. My foster mother picked me up from the hospital and took me to her home in Willow Spring. She took photos of me, fed me, gave me my pain medication. She placed me in a crate with fresh kibble and water. She exercised me several times a day, and taught me to potty outside. Melissa and Glenn were also fostering a big yellow lab named Ben. He liked me and I liked him. The couple also owned their own labs, Jeter and Uma, and we all lived together in the Williford home. The best thing she did was give me a soft stuffed dog to sleep with, and a warm blanket. She put a pretty pink collar around my neck, and I was proud of myself. I liked my foster mother. When my foster father came home that night from work, he held me, and patted me. I felt his strength and his love. I liked my foster father, too. He really loved me; I felt it.

Carson Williford

I met and loved my foster folks' granddaughter, Carson. She told me she loved me, and she hugged and kissed me a lot. Carson even drew a picture of me! I was happy that Carson drew my picture.

My foster mother posted my name, photos, a video, and description on PLR's website for adoption on January 31, 2019. I spent ten wonderful days living with the Willifords. The glowing and warming light was always near me, comforting me, and I knew that someday, and in some way, I would find my way to a final destination. It would be a place I would call home, and with a family who would love me.

On February 1, 2019, my foster mother received numerous emails from folks who were interested in a "Greet and Meet" session with me for my potential adoption. Three people contacted my foster mother. The policy for PLR adoption, is the first one who called the foster, and had also completed a form, and paid a registration fee would meet me first.

The first candidate to meet the requirements is writing my story for me.

She set up an appointment on Friday, February 1, 2019, with my foster folks. She and her husband came to meet and greet me, and the Willifords the next day, Saturday, February 2 at their home, and mine in Willow Spring, North Carolina. They drove up to their house and pulled into the driveway, and right away the lady jumped out of the pick-up truck, and ran to the fence around the backyard where my foster parents and I were relaxing, enjoying the afternoon. She introduced herself and her husband to my foster parents, and then my foster mother picked me up and showed me to the lady. They came into the backyard and the lady took me and held me, and cuddled me. I felt happy to have so many people like me. We all left the backyard and went inside to the kitchen area. The lady and my foster mother sat down at the kitchen table to look at papers, and then the lady signed a paper. She wrote my foster mother a check, and she said,

"I am purchasing this puppy for my birthday, which is a week from today." I was a birthday present! My foster mother took pictures of me with the couple, and somehow I knew that I was going somewhere with them, and I was leaving my home of ten days with my foster parents. Once again, my chest was thumping, and I was frightened.

Glenn and Melissa Williford

Josie and Papa

The couple took me to their pick-up truck, and the lady kept me in her lap, and we drove off, waving good-bye to my fosters. I began to feel sad, and I whimpered, and then cried. I wanted to stay with the Willifords and their furry friends. The lady who was holding me, hugged me, and said, "It's going to be okay. You'll see. We are taking you to Virginia to your forever and ever and ever home. I promise that we will care for you, and love you for the rest of your life. You will never be abandoned or abused again. This is your final stop!" She held me close, and cuddled me and my raggedy stuffed dog, my fosters had given me. And, then she said, "Your new and forever name is Josie, my dear puppy." I wouldn't get the hang of that name until much later. My name was now Josie Eastwood!

We drove to another lady's house in North Carolina. It was the couple's daughters' home. We went inside the house, and this lady liked me, too. She picked me up, and cuddled me, and my new father stretched out on the sofa with me on his chest, and I really liked it. While we were snuggling, his mobile phone rang, and it was my foster mother. She called to tell my new family that she had forgotten to give them my pain medication. So, we left, and drove to a shopping center, and met my foster mother and her daughter. She gave my new mother my pain medication, and we were off to a place called Virginia.

During the long drive to Virginia, I got really sleepy. In the backseat of the truck was a brand new bed and blanket, and a stuffed animal. It was all just for me. My new mama placed me in the bed, and I liked it, but I liked being held in her arms more. So, I slept in her lap until we finally arrived at what would be my new and forever and ever home; a place called Keeling, Virginia.

This couple gathered me and my things together and took me into the house. It was very dark outside, quite late. I could still see the light that had been with me since I was left abandoned in the woods in Cumberland County, North Carolina. It followed us into the house. The light had followed me to Virginia.

My new mama and daddy put my bed in a nice corner in the kitchen with my new blanket and my toys. They put me down, and I looked around my new home. It was warm, and it felt like home. However, another creature met me and my new folks in the kitchen, and that creature they introduced to me as their cat, Woo Woo. Woo Woo did not like me, however he did learn to tolerate me. We had an understanding, that he had seniority; "top dog," my new mama claimed, even though he was a cat.

The days passed, and after many accidents of losing my manners, and not making it to the potty pads in the kitchen, I learned to ask to go outside to do what nature called me to do. My new family taught me a lot of fun things to do, and I learned quickly that tricks and other things that they asked me to do would earn treats. Those treats were quite tasty. Sometimes I felt like grabbing Mama's pants leg, and shaking it. I also did a lot of teething on Mama's hand, and sometimes she would yip like me, when it hurt. I soon learned not to bite her hand. She told me it was okay to mouth her, but not bite.

Then one day, I noticed that the light who had been with me since the beginning of my journey was fading out, and not as bright as it had once been. I asked the light, "What are you?" The light answered, "I am Passage." "Passage?" I questioned. "What is that?" The light flickered and replied, "I am your passage, and no other's. Your will to live, and keep going, when all odds were against you, summoned me to fill your heart with warmth to keep you, and sustain you, until you no longer needed it.

You are home, dear puppy girl, and you have a name, your name on a dangling heart, on a brand new red collar loving placed around your neck.

You are now a member of a wonderful family, your family, to care for you and love you forever, and "furever!"

Passage continued, "My time is up, and I must leave you, Josie. Always remember your journey, and love those who helped you along the way. Lavish them with slobbery kisses and big snuggles. You are blessed. Be a blessing in return." Then passage dimmed until it disappeared. Passage was gone. But, I felt good, for I knew that I was finally home, and I would live with a family, and be happy.

Passage, the bright and warm light above my head was gone. However, now I felt that warming light inside of my chest.

In the days to come, I discovered that my new home was a big farm named "Turkey Roost," so named in homage to the many wild turkey that called my farm home, as well. Our farm is located in a very rural community. There are acres and acres of land to do what any dog loves to do; run free, jump, chase, swim in the pond, and splash in the creeks; and just horse around. And, that was a good thing because when I met my new vets and friends, Dr. Lisa and Dr. Victoria, new X-rays showed that my leg had healed on its own. I did not need surgery. The vet in Apex and my new vets agreed it was healed, and it was a miracle! Mama and Daddy said that I was a miracle!

Josie & Wyatt

And, my new folks loved me so very much that they decided to adopt another Labrador from PLR. And, in March 2019 they adopted a boy puppy named Baron. My folks renamed him Wyatt. I now had a brother, Wyatt, who is a Labrador Retriever. I have celebrated my first and second birthdays with my family. On my very first birthday, we had cake with red candles and vanilla ice cream. On the cake written in red icing were the words Happy Birthday Josie.

Life is good and I am happy. Passage lives inside of my heart.

I run in fields of wheat and tall grasses. I swim in the farm pond. I explore the big creek that runs through the land. I play with my favorite toy, my red Kong ball. I chase Wyatt and he chases me. We both run after the whitetails on our farm. We ride with Daddy in the farm pick-up truck to take the household trash to the community waste deposit theater. We accompany Daddy when he visits others and run errands in our family pick-up truck. At night we bed down in the den on the sofa, and we each have our own blanket. Life is wonderful, for I am now an important member of a family.

There are so many canines waiting for you to adopt them, joining them with your family. Consider this, my true story. I promise you will never be disappointed in the unconditional love you, and yours will be given freely from the heart of the dog you adopt. As they say, "Don't shop, adopt."

I say this to you, truly, the relationship between a human being, and their canine companion can be a bond like none other. Reach out and touch the heart of a dog today.

Everyone loves a good dog story, and there are so many more stories that are longing to be told.

THE END

Animal Urgent Care Fayetteville, NC

19 Jan

Injured puppy (estimated 8 wks old) is picked up on road side by "good samaritans" in Fayetteville, NC, no nearby residential areas, is taken to Animal Urgent Care

Cumberland County Animal Control Fayetteville, NC

19 Jan

Fayetteville Police Department was called to transfer puppy from Animal Urgent Care to Cumberland County Animal Control

Peak Lab Rescue Apex, NC

22 Jan

Peak Lab Rescue commits to rescue, transports from Cumberland County Animal Control, naming her "Sasha" Posts on PLR Foster Families Facebook

2019

Harmony Animal Hospital Apex, NC

22 Jan

"Sasha" admitted to Harmony Animal Hospital "Sasha" is fostered by Melissa & Glenn Willford Willow Spring, NC "Sasha" is posted for adoption on Jan 31, 2019

2019 Keeling, Virginia

2 Feb

Celebrate! "Sasha" is adopted by Judi & John Eastwood Keeling Virginia "Sasha" is renamed "Josie"

~ Afterword ~

Though our beloved Josie's severely injured leg healed on its own, which is truly miraculous, she continues to struggle with the trauma imposed upon her at just eight weeks old. Though we do not know the extent of the abuse she suffered, we do know that it was dreadful.

To date, our Josie continues to experience night terrors during her sleeping time. Sometimes when she is riding with us in the truck, dark wooded areas trigger severe bouts of trembling and attempts to hide on the floorboard of the truck. She is overly possessive of food and her red ball. During her first summer with us, it took her three months before she would get into the farm pond. Once she learned that she was born to swim and to retrieve, she was a natural; a graceful swimmer and excellent at retrieving a ball tossed into the water.

Josie is terrified of ascending and descending the stairs; our thought that falling down the stairs may be how she broke her leg. She has recently, on her own, mastered her fear of coming up the basement steps, and we are so very happy for her.

It is challenging to work with her at times. However, we are patient, kind, understanding, consistent in praising her and disciplining her, and all of the love we hold for her in our hearts is more than enough to get her through difficult times.

Josie is amazingly intelligent, understanding human language, words and their meanings. She opens the kitchen door to let herself out. She fetches my coat off of the hall rack when I ride with Daddy, Wyatt and her on outings. We spent last summer exploring our creek, and if I was lagging behind Daddy, Wyatt and her, she would come back and stay with me until I caught up. Once, she helped me get up a steep bank at the bridge culvert to get out. I held onto her collar and she backed up and pulled me out. She loves to give us slobbery kisses and snuggles. She wakes Daddy in the morning with gentle snuggles and kisses, laying her head in his lap, reaching to lick his face, asking to go outside to potty.

There are just not enough pages that I can write to tell all who read this, what an amazing canine our Josie is.

Our family celebrates the gift of Josie everyday. We look forward to sharing in her life in the coming years. We know that Josie is happy, for she demonstrates her happiness each time we go to the creek, ride in the truck, play games, and when it is snack time, during quiet time in the evenings.

It is my hope that Josie's Passage will inspire readers to consider adoption of rescued dogs, and to welcome them into your families with the love and family life they deserve.

Mission Statement of Peak Lab Rescue: Finding permanent homes for Labs and Lab Mixes rescued from abuse, neglect, abandonment, and high-kill shelters throughout North Carolina. Peak Lab Rescue is the largest foster-based dog rescue in North Carolina, which means they do not have a facility. All Peak Labs live in foster homes where they learn the skills necessary to become successful family members.

Profits from sales of this book will be donated to Peak Lab Rescue in honor of Josie Eastwood.

For more information on helping Peak Lab Rescue in the continuation of rescuing and providing care for Labs and Lab Mixes visit…

peaklabrescue.com

John and Judi Eastwood

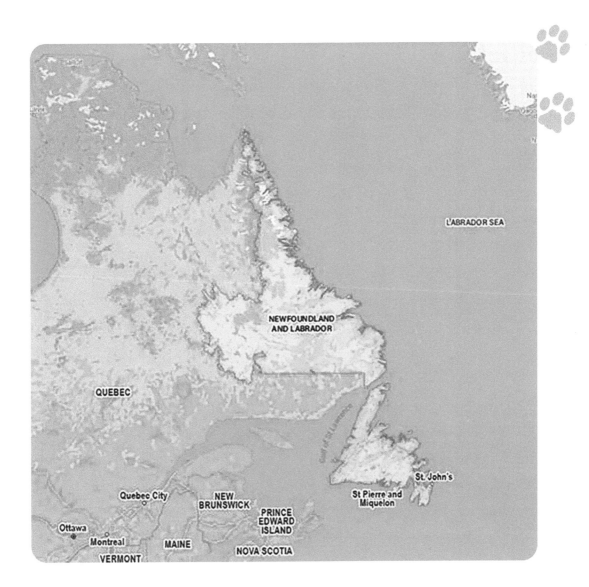

History of the Labrador Retriever

In the beginning, my ancestors originated in Newfoundland, in the 1500s. Newfoundland, Labrador, and the Sea of Labrador are located on the coast of Canada. During that period, Newfoundlands were bred with a dog called the St. John's Water-dog or Lesser Newfoundland. These dogs were owned by fisherman. They bravely jumped into icy waters to retrieve fish, which had fallen off the hook, or help drag in large nets filled with fish. These dogs were great at their job, because their oily coats repelled water and their webbed paws made them excellent swimmers. The climate and weather conditions in Newfoundland were harsh. The St. John's Water-dog was the ancestor of today's Labrador Retriever.

27

The role of these dogs, as the name suggests, were being at home in the water, as much or more, than the land. They proved to excel in retrieving nets, lines and ropes. They dove underwater to retrieve fish that had slipped off the hooks. They were highly valued by their human companions and worked hard to please their owners.

These dogs were then brought to England in the early 1800s. They became very popular with hunters, as well as fisherman. The dogs were used in shooting sports and their owners began to call them "Labradors," named for the region of Labrador and its sea. The name remained and by 1903, Labradors were recognized by the English Kennel Club.

Labradors were capturing the attention of hunters and farmers in the United States of America. The American Kennel Club recognized the breed, Labrador Retriever in 1917.

By the beginning of the twentieth century, the St. John's Water-dog was becoming extinct. The last of the St. John's Water-dog died in the 1980s.

However, this breed of dog left us a legacy that would give us the most popular dog breed in the world; the amazing and beloved breed, the Labrador Retriever.

This breed is the most popular pet dog in the United States of America, the United Kingdom, and the most valued working retriever in the world.

I am Josie, and I am proud of the heritage that is mine to tell. I am happy that I was born a Labrador Retriever, and "Passage" is now in my heart.

CPSIA information can be obtained
at www.ICGtesting.com
Printed in the USA
BVHW021801300822
645851BV00016B/635

9 781643 147147